Blue Rose

ALSO BY THE AUTHOR

As Carol Muske-Dukes

POETRY

Sparrow

Twin Cities

FICTION

Dear Digby

Saving St. Germ

Life After Death

Channeling Mark Twain

ESSAYS

Married to the Icepick Killer: A Poet in Hollywood

ANTHOLOGY

Crossing State Lines: An American Renga (coedited with Bob Holman)

As Carol Muske

POETRY

Camouflage

Skylight

Wyndmere

Applause

Red Trousseau

An Octave Above Thunder

ESSAYS

Women and Poetry: Truth, Autobiography, and the Shape of the Self

Blue Rose

Carol Muske-Dukes

PENGUIN POETS

PENGUIN BOOKS

An imprint of Penguin Random House LLC
375 Hudson Street
New York, New York 10014
penguin.com

LIBRARY OF CONGRESS CATALOGING-IN-PUBLICATION DATA

Names: Muske-Dukes, Carol, 1945– author.
Title: Blue rose / Carol Muske-Dukes.
Description: New York : Penguin Books, 2018. | Series: Penguin poets
Identifiers: LCCN 2017044268 (print) | LCCN 2017045712 (ebook) |
ISBN 9781524705015 (e-book) | ISBN 9780143131250 (paperback)
Subjects: | BISAC: POETRY / American / General.
Classification: LCC PS3563.U837 (ebook) | LCC PS3563.U837 A6 2018 (print) |
DDC 811/.54—dc23
LC record available at https://lccn.loc.gov/2017044268

Printed in the United States of America
1 3 5 7 9 10 8 6 4 2

Set in Adobe Garamond Premier Pro   ·   Designed by Elke Sigal

For my daughter,
Annie Muske-Dukes (Driggs)
—and in memory of my mother and father
—and for Jane Mead: brave phoenix,
rising from the ashes

Contents

III.

IV.

Gold, blood, ivory, shadow—
Like the one in his hands, invisible rose.
—Jorge Luis Borges, "A Rose and Milton"

I.

Blue Rose

She came too fast: couldn't slow
my body's unstoppable intent
till the EMTs shouted how. I

flashed on the driver's fast-calculating
eyes in the dash mirror as he amped
the siren overhead. Later, lashed to

a pallet, I glimpsed the sky: a dawn
moon intact before the rapid hands of
a hospital clock. In the labor room, she

crowned, then turned, withdrawing from
this world, as if she'd glimpsed its fixed,
monolithic white. Entering light, she was

danger blue, yet to me her color appeared
something never imagined: if-flower of myth,
bloom on the isle of the color-blind, far

from our spectrum. Red to magenta to a breath
of cyan. So there were just her eyelids, bruised
as new petals. Just her brain's opening rose.

The morning sky, turning a color never before seen.

Live/Die: a Ghazal

—Elsie Kuchera Muske, 1916–2015

The door of the hospice room in which you die
stays open. Dreaming, you drift there, dying

in that floating bed of fierce arguments that live
on, until the moment when you no longer live.

Cheered on by a chorus of voices as you die,
"Go now! Go to the light!" Still, Don't die!

cries a dissenting voice within: a flickering live
wire behind the night-light's angel face. Live

news at 7 A.M., after the great orange moon dies.
Sunlight fingers a blue bowl of shaved ice. Die?

No. Not now. A tiny version of you pops out alive
from a burning wood, swims upstream, panting. Lively

as Nurse Good's soft-shoe entrance to applause, dying.
She smiles, squints at her syringe, held up, lit, like dye

bubbles lengthening in a radiant corridor: see lives
unborn (half souls blindly pushing toward life)

gather outside time, inside your mind. Move! Die!
they cry. You won't acquiesce. Mother, I cannot die

for you, I don't know how. You brought me here alive.
You taught me everything but how to let you die.

Orphanage

Awake suddenly and afraid, I looked down from my
high window into the spinning prism of snow, past
the new flattened macadam to the white meadow below.

I watched the drifts cover the tall grass, where in
summer, rabbits and whip-poor-wills hid from eager
slingshots, in family-size plots following the surveyors'

black flags. I'd been awakened by a sound: something
stuck, spinning its wheels. A truck, I could see now, as
it lunged suddenly out of the deep rut it had made trying

to downshift at the top of the meadow path leading to
the orphanage below. As the truck lurched free, I could see
its tailgate shudder, gape, then a quick cascade of tumbling

shapes. Taillights, bright red blurs, vanishing.
Moonlit, my school coat and scarf drawn on, I
went spinning down through the sleeping house:

feeling its familiar steady rebuke. Slipping out, ghostly
in blowing snow, I found them where they'd fallen.
Dolls. A scattered family, lying faceup, eyes staring

past me at the sky as their silly faces were slowly erased.
Kewpie-pouts, clumsy spit-curls. Raggedy Ann dresses,
cheaply made. As if a collection taken at the new church

nearby had paid a doll factory to spin off a poor version
of something lovable. Special delivery. Though now I
heard a chime. It must have been Christmas. It must have

been hours before the nuns led their small charges out to
salt the ice and shovel the hill where others sledded. They
honored the earth: I'd watched how their gardens grew

lush in summer, all the way to the iron gates. I thought how
soon they would be gone, along with the living meadow.
So why have I kept close for years this dream of them, coming

upon the tossed dolls, face after unloved face, in the bright
new morning? Holding them tight all the way home. Though
there was no home, of course: I knew there never was one.

No Hands

He rode "no hands," speeding
headlong down the hill near
our house, his arms extended,
held rigid away from his body,
our small daughter behind him
on the bike in her yellow sunsuit,
bareheaded. She held on to him
for her life. I watched them from
above—helpless: a failed brake.
Far below us, a stop-sign rose
like a child's toy shield. He could
not stop, he would not. That hunger
for display overrode danger, illusions
of safety. Even death had less to do
with it than the will's eventual triumph
over stasis: how he'd finally fly free
and how she might accompany him,
as an audience travels with a performer,
an object of regard. Downward, fast—
so what cannot stop holds on, holds on
to a mind flying away from itself, seeking
release from the soul speeding away, yet
staying close as breath, even at this distance.

Rain

"Rain Room is an immersive environment of perpetually falling
water that pauses wherever a human body is detected."
—Los Angeles County Museum of Art

"Here you have no rain, when all the earth cries for it."
—Mary Austin, *The Land of Little Rain*, 1903

Bride after towering L.A. bride: whirl-tops, their
headdresses switchblading the hot August wind!

Transplanted palms, wrote Mary Austin, are *Young wives,
abandoned—slowly grasping that all marriages go dry . . .*

Could she have imagined water in tiers, engineered in
drought? *We're looking at the end of known weather.*

Each cell of cloudburst held above each human body.
Real fake rain, real fake feeling. Does all water, falling,

smell like regret? Where nostalgia parks its dark
apothecary? Where that glass wand, once dipped

in a chemist's vial, slides silvery distillate called
Rain, fragrant handcuffs over each pulse. Downpour

in a dream oil—the corner pharmacy gone famous.
Even pimps slapped it on, as they hunkered together

back then, outside the Women's House of D. That
cagey scent edging out blue gusts of rolled grass.

Same *Rain* in incarcerated air: its cranked-up heat
& Muzak. When I brought the prisoners books of

poems, they slipped me scribbled phone numbers:
Please call to check if my baby in a new foster.

I called, I kept calling. My jeans jacket spilling
dollars & quarters from the Women's Bail Fund

at the half-cranked window on the Rock. Pregnancy
our 1st priority. $50, $75. Mothers first. New York to

L.A. pimps their women prisoners. Unreal walls within
real walls. A wild deluge, framed inside the space

you are now free to exit, meta-wet. Each guard station: single
file. Arc lights, kleig-lit desert sun. Poems scribbled on paper

scraps after hours in labor. *Drenched*, she wrote, *shackled to steel bed.*
My baby taken a ward of state. Where long ago it was pointed

out, these limits of desire, then birth. Mary Austin's
streets of palms: transplanted, like Novalis's blue flowers,
                              wards of a golden state.

Then the contractions start: nothing can hold them back.

Ferris Wheel

Driving westward, the freeway lit by sun-in-smoke,
wildfire sky. Unsummoned, a kid's waking dream
of a great wheel, all seats filled by personal gods:

the laughing jackal face, the thunderbird mother of
night, sure-shot madonna, horror-boys & my fave, Janus—
all rocking in thought-cradles above the swan boats at

the bottom. Where the brakeman in the Peter Pan bandanna
(hiding his chemo-bald head) keeps the whole swirl running.
Stop spinning like that   the long ago voices called to me. I,

undiagnosed. I kept turning like a top, within sound spinning
outward from the diamond tooth of a Zenith snake, that needle-
arm on vinyl lines. Now that Blue Danube score flows so fast that

the wheel cranks backward. Clouds part to reveal a holiness-in-snow,
thrown up. How I knelt in terror, dawn mass past, nine & saintish-mad,
about to cover the sacred wafer in icy white with these very hands now

clutching the lock-bar as we keep on rocking. More clouds, pink-lit like lip-
prints of the dying on glass, mirror. Lovers & trusted few once next to me,
"forever & ever" till they closed the coffin lids. Fire-on-fire like maternal
      circular logic

I followed away from the catechism god whose first proof was that he existed, while she grew faster on pagan heights. Assassins, developers, woman-killers, don't know from the palindrome of this hurt earth. So double-gazing Janus

stands up, risks falling off, to say s/he saw this coming. Look how flames have overtaken fairgrounds here. Pay no attention to these fireworks revealing a sky's lit-up gears, machine-y in its glass-tight interior. Stand on

renegade heaven & turn—write it forth & back, as is just—

just keep turning.

Kashmir: Hindu Doctor

I walked down a side street in Srinagar. All of them side streets,
under chenar trees, as ancient as the shadows of the brooding
Himalayas. The River Jhelum had stopped flooding now,
after days of rain. British houseboats rode low on Dal Lake.

The floating peddlers went on singing like waterbirds at dawn—
their small skiffs heaped with treasure from Tibetan temples.
Three hundred miles from China: robbers, singing about
their loot. I found the clinic by following a line: women in
hijabs, walking behind their husbands. The men raised loud voices,
complaining. They grew silent at the clinic door, stepping aside slowly,

as their wives entered. The doctor signaled to me over their veiled heads.
She was "Hindi," therefore hated. A woman: therefore hated. A doctor:
respectful hate. Me, I believed in medical help. I'd seen the U.N. trucks,
the Red Cross carrying out the bodies of the flood-dead. *It was necessary
to intervene now.* I sat with my notebook writing down what the doctor did.

Outside, the men had begun to shout again. They knew their wives
would stand naked in her gaze. Breathing bare beneath her metal disk. *Breathe.*
A sound like wind howling. A woman slowly unwrapped herself, becoming
a naked female body in a long mirror. I looked at unformed forms afloat in bottles.
Green glass pillars: elixirs, shot with sudden sun. A wall map of hated India.
They come when the pain compels them to come, she said as she felt breasts,
drew a quick blue-black path on a torso to be followed in surgery. The
men hunkered on prayer rugs outside. Witchcraft, they were saying. People
believed these things. But sometimes it was just sewing a body up again, too late.
Needles full of relief, handfuls of pain stoppers. A photograph I took of her didn't
make the magazine. When she took a break, past dusk, I walked out with her.

Men whose wives rested inside murmured at her, then sang out complicated curses. I had my quote: *They come when the pain compels them.* When is it necessary to intervene. I believe in medical help. There was a smell of blood, I thought, but blood doesn't smell. I'd missed how a thrown rock had opened an old scar just above her eye. She laughed, singsong, drew a veil over her face.

Kept walking.

Requiem for a Requiem

—Paula Modersohn-Becker, 1876–1907

Shaking shame from her brush, she presses
it to canvas. Before her, women could not
paint women naked, could not
gaze into the mirror of their flesh.

Still lifes erasing taboo: spite-green goblet,
halved fruit. The women staring, bare. Or
nursing unclothed, eyes on the artist's eyes.
                                   Without shame: a style.

She haunts her friend, Rilke, from beyond
the grave she predicted for herself, days past
giving birth. For years: refused that death

warrant. Near the art colony, she reinvents
her solitude. Glass held up to query an angle,
bootlegged light in a doorway. Bootlegged:

a daughter's open eyes. Clichés of haunt: Paris
ateliers, Cézanne's oranges, fractured Picasso
nudes. Knowing what they knew. Saw how

style derives from itself: how a body idealized
by desire floats in trees, vanishes in clouds.
Never to laugh, pick up a kid, bleed. She picks

up a kid, bleeds. Leaving Rilke's portrait un-
done. Drifting now into his "Requiem,"
writ for her: "friend," this shadow body, he

beckons now into candlelight. She listens
to her own breath, dying. So like each
gasp at the start. Says: *Did you know Death*

cheers at each conception? as Love looks to her
in the mirror: sweet murder. Chance-
implacable is the enthroned soul, rising on

each brushstroke. Deathless: a woman's body.
But "Schande!" she cries, her dying
word, holding her newborn daughter to her breast.

Shame! *Soul, come claim the body.*

Failure to Thrive

O the body's much ballyhoo'd right to be born!
Aligning with her right to shine & die, a star!
They all know her name but not her age
a doctor our daughters shared, opined.

Her name, he said, was famous, but a failure.
(Thrived on-screen, you've seen her.)
My daughter towered above her in real
life. Born on the same day back then, they

might notice you at the edge of the field
with your banners and bottled cells.
A managed tot, from the womb unstoppered,

brained up for the stupids. Don't grow!
Don't rise into big citizenship! Soul underling,
soul malingering at the gate! Till the end of the

body's time: Unicorn, my little porn. Wanted
to unhunger her too, I. But she filled the screen
in that field of dying flowers. Famous-eyed,
turned away from the gift of sustenance, brave: no
semblance of a future beyond everyone's fake-maternal mind.

Liars' banners. Then the unicorn's passage: lightfoot.
And so loved, lightfoot, so apparently loved:
Some of us must starve in order to be seen.

Audition

—Paris, *Hair*, 1971

Once through an ancient stage door, past a sign
L'audition, I'm ushered by hip Mercury, cocked

torch lighting his winged brow. My number's the one
he hands me, though I don't know how: to act or

if I can belt "Easy to Be Hard." Which I do.
How can people be so heartless? I ask the high

notes. The day before I'd quoted de Beauvoir with
equal fire as a Metro creep touched my leg, crooning,

flat. I shouted back my textbook "Va t'on!" which he
instantly corrected. My error: *wrong person familiar.* Now

an anonymous voice from a dark row: asking for one
more number: later a callback at my Cité U dorm.

Suddenly onstage, piping high notes at a Hell's
Angel, missing back-of-chorus cues, half-rehearsed.

The first bars of "Aquarius" chime & I climb, hand
over hand, from scaffolding below the side balconies

into scripted light. But the Tribe didn't take to me.
The only time I took my clothes off at the nude scene,

Act I's end: they hid my tie-dyed jeans. I couldn't be
naked the way they were. I think everything is real.

Nude all interlude, I searched behind the great
moth-eaten sway of cloth, beneath hanging skies.

In my forever-auditioning blond body, begging in each
failed language: "My clothes?" "Pourquoi, mes amis?"

Funny joke, but these bright fake tryouts at Life, ongoing,
take a toll. Due to be paid up, up Mercury's road. Everything

was real to me, even the ongoing joke war over a woman's body.
What I shout back exiting is how I believe it will all come down—

in a future when She, Great Moon, rises up, floods the Seventh
House, & Jupiter aligns peacefully at last, with his partner, Mars.

The Year the Law Changed

Waiting hours, each of us in a curtain-stall.
Two men outside, mopping the floor and hall,
Shouting "Murderers!" at us. Were they janitors?
Or medics who'd read our charts & diagnosed?
If men could get pregnant, it would end up
a sacrament, Gloria said. Simone said *We
know that no woman takes it lightly. So
could both be true.* In class in San Francisco
our teacher spoke of his wife who lost
a child to leukemia, haunted by her ghost
& told by her shrink to write about blood.
She wrote about a vampire and her book shot
to fame so maybe she forgot the one who
never grew into her name. When my name
was called I went to have it done and then knew
I had my life back but covered myself with blood—
mine and some not—but still of me. I don't know
what I mean by "of me," it's undefined & even
the shouting accusers won't cross that line. I had to
swear I was clinically mad to have it done. What's
madness to the men in white: they clean the world
of residue like me and all the blood from both of us.

II.

Coolbrith

I was used to the wind, those long billow-topped months,

hard path wind that built & scattered its alphabet of longing.
The wind took the bridles, straining the way the horses
leaned up now into strange new air, their nostrils quaking.

As we crossed over the pass, Beckwourth brought me up
from the back to the lead schooners as they shuddered
up the rise. He was a black man, a frontiersman, free as I
would be freed, my mother shielding her eyes in the sun:

"Go ahead now, Coolbrith." My old name fell from me into
canyon shadows, never to be spoken again while I lived.
Standing at the summit, I am no longer the child of dead
prophets. I am his child with his sight: the circling redtail

drifting over the Sierras. My kingdom, he said, because he
knew me to be highborn, not in name but in namelessness.
He waved his hand over the valley below, calling to the others

that it was here, what we'd come for—here, now: *California*.

Coolbrith: Homage

—Ina Coolbrith (née Josephine Donna Smith), 1841–1928,
First Poet Laureate, State of California

"What would happen if one woman told the truth about her life?
The world would split open."
—Muriel Rukeyser

That oath sworn & kept till her deathbed. The poet
unseals at the end: revealing how her mother was
wed in secret to the Prophet Smith, her dead husband's

brother. Josephine Donna Smith turns on her last pillow
toward a locked past, her mind still married to contradiction:
endless flight from polygamy, from the prophet's mob murder.
A mother's command, each child blood-sworn, her maiden
name a cover, a Coolbrith.

Never speak of this. Dying, that twice-named girl restores
it all: the way their wagons at last crested the Sierras.
She stands there next to the black frontiersman,
Beckwourth, as he points through clouds. Crown
upon floating crown circling lazily down to sun
reddening the Pacific. His gesture: "Your kingdom."

But what she writes: *How bright the sunset glory
lies! Its radiance spans the western skies!* Summit
pass, his hand on her shoulder, a hawkwing ablaze in
"western skies." Words emptying words. Another immigrant
soul, circling. Another woman in flight. Sun sliding down

inside its fallen bloodred crown. Below, indigenous
children unlearning their native tongue, reciting mission
Spanish: *El Pueblo de Nuestra Senora la Reyna de Los Angeles.*
Virgin queen, mother of immigrants, of orphans. To fear
            being erased yet embracing erasure:
                                    Welcome! Welcome! Western skies!

Welcome Ina Coolbrith: teenage "Sweet Singer" on
the *L.A. Star*'s poetry page, its far-flung society page.
(Her fiancé, a thug from the ironworks.) How do wedding
vows rescue an oath sworn against that union?
Imagine her: swerving from a fist in the face, gunfire
from that white drunk in blackface. Vigilante minstrel.
In her arms, the now-silent baby. But she mask-writes:

To-day—ah, baby mine—to-day God holds
thee in His keeping! And yet I weep, as one pale
ray breaks in upon thy sleeping . . .

Call it immigrant terror: half-public hidden life.
Escaping upcoast, alone, childless—she beards
Joaquin Miller by the bay. His half-Indian daughter,
adopted as her own. Hiding in plain sight
those encoded lives, *Ah, baby mine.* Bret Harte,
Mark Twain, John Muir—maybe-lovers who
made her their Gold Rush La Passionata:
                                    Oakland Librarian!

"Sentimental verse," but what burned
            just beneath her dreaming stanzas.

She writes:

> ... *saw the Gate burn*
> *in the sunset the thin thread of mist creeps white across*
> *the Sausalito hills* ...
> ("Commonplace," sniffed a
> New York critic.)

But *Welcome!* Hired as Reception at the Bohemian Club,
where Great Men pissed on redwoods, waltzing two by two
in drop-dead drag. She wrote:
> *The secrets of the field, My blossoms*
> *will not yield* ...

My blossoms will not yield—the sealed chambers, oath &
vow. Till another now: she is California Poet Laureate,

Local headlines call her home. By rail, in the late path
of the prairie schooner, rocking. Girl-child reading Byron:

I pluck the laurel crown! It ripened in the western breeze ...

I wore her laurel crown as an actor-governor mimed
crowning himself, inside his smoking tent outside state
offices. *Welcome!* the signs said, an arrow pointing

to that pitched space where he joked, off-the-
boat showman: puffing, *What are your poems about?*

Laughed-at accent. Stogie-stacked ashtray. His
own arrival, lifting things. Unlike the way she came.
(Dying oxen swept off, fording the deep river.
Drowning bellows in her head, half a century gone.)

Yet rising up again he takes her hand, welcoming official—
As long ago, she danced fandango with Pio Pico, Mayor of
the vaquero town of Los Angeles. Here on earthquake terrain:
            unstoppable poppies, anybody's Pacific!

Later, memory's bloodred petals up-drifting, suspended in wind.
Door-slam. He flings himself in, roaring, shoots out windows.
         She holds the baby to her heart. Too late to flee.

Fleeing, she's Coolbrith of Russian Hill,
      Overland Monthly, Bohemian soirees—
      She: charter member of a gesture,
          in her masked diction. *Too late to flee.*

But she sees *"the Gate burn"*—& for a moment
his face in the fire: *"Beautiful scout,"* former slave,
             declaring her queen.

What are your poems about? he asks,
his mask-face floating up over other smoke-faces.
Say "California," where flight ends?
           or *California:*

Meaning a woman, a woman's life.
Resistance. A tent, a wall.

Or—past burning gates:
her tent cities, her wildfires, border watch, her sanctuaries.
California, Governor, where we're all

welcomed in the name of *La Reina de Nada*:
names circled in entry documents,
stacked up in smoke—
where she paused, looking at her life in code—
signed twice-invisible,
then signed on the line: *Coolbrith.*

Adrienne

—In memoriam, Adrienne Rich, 1929–2012

After the funeral, her voice on the phone.
Your husband did not want to die, she said. *Mine did.*
What's the same is that you must survive no matter what.
Back then, there was a lot of "no matter what" & I learned
who my friends were & learned my crazy strength. I learned
from her. She kept moving after he took his life but used
the headboard image, a single gravestone above two bodies
in bed, holding them together even as they broke apart. She
carried that headboard through snow, in a poem about moving house.
Of marriage ended by death, she opened a new path: *"I live now not*
as a leap / but a succession of brief, amazing movements / each one
making possible the next." Carried that steady voice in my head, then
recalled hearing it long before, beside me, as we climbed together up
an icy rise to a women's prison where I'd invited her to read. She was
limping badly & carried a cane even then—but I was too timid to
reach out to help her along. I feared her fearlessness, her anger &
impatient struggle forward—yet she was so small & bent & the slippery up-
hill ascent so daunting I began to offer my hand. Then saw her set expression in
snowy arc-light. Heard her urging herself on, as in the poem. Step
after step, forward & up: each powerful act of will making possible the next.

A Girl's Guide to the Epic

Arms & the woman, I sing...
—West Point, 1997

We stopped at the sound of a sister-voice, calling out
on the Plain. "Ten Hut!" My daughter & I stood at the edge

of the parade: waves of file-gray flashing by. Who was
she up close? I read my poems to the same gray plebe sea.

A boy called Charlie Foxtrot Tango Bravo raised his hand.
Had I always hated men? Sure! I mugged & the 18 percent

cheered in their higher register. I referenced Athena, gray-eyed,
springing from that furrowed god-brow. *Ma'am? That is a metaphor,*

ma'am! Tangled in the rosy fingers of dawn & the wine-dark
sea, her voice wavering, often lost as plunder is lost & yet kept,

grief recorded as siren call. *Ma'am?* If war burns down
your town—how are you to tell the mast-lashed bards from

the warlords? Had I always hated men? *It's a joke, son.* How to
describe her desire (for what?) after she leapt out, fully-armed.

Later, in plebe Lit, I heard it repeated, how "Conscience
makes cowards of us all" ... *is a metaphor?* Fierce,

the new voice on an ancient Plain. Yet Sappho turns
her back on Lydian warriors, tall ships. *I say it is what one
loves.* We spotted her: Brava, Foxtrot Charlie. & looked for

Poe in the cemetery, found Custer. Edgar Allan wouldn't march
or drill. A gambler, sacked. Wild west wind blew up, on its own,

from the same dawn. (Weil called it "Poem of Force.") Same old voice.

Weil

Joan was burned as a cross-dresser, not a warrior
for the wimpy Dauphin. The Maid of Orleans turned
to ash in a ladies' shift. When Weil went on the factory

floor, she'd also abandoned female drag. Invisible in breeches,
unadorned armor like La Pucelle, who rose to glory dressed in
smoke. Even the field lilies bowed to it, martyrdom's theater,

red-hot wind on the spectacle of torch. Young Simone was no
martyr, she sought the deeper grave below the rack & stake . . .
the nature of unhappiness: to which a residue of mystery will

always cling. In queue to witness the place within the body
where *shame arrests lamentation*—her gaze on an old woman's
hands or "weariness . . . in the set of a mouth." Where the sun comes

up: a punch clock. Shame's whip raising scars on a plodder's back.
Her mind refusing abstraction. Her bread, her clock, her pencil—
prying open the soul's depths. She wakes. Window shades rattle

in a migraine wind, daily pain. Her desire to punch someone
in the mirror spot of her own headache. Counterclockwise
goes the slot-in of each day's time-slight. Set at random for

somebody's mercy. A break for bread, coffee, a fever-brow
touched once by the wide-open mind of a mystic working stiff.

Ekphrasis

Homer was in love with Achilles'
shield & sang to it. Vulcan pounded
in the world, double ply, silver strap.
The Iliad, Book 18, is where we get the

picture: the blacksmith's management
of a trendy Hell, with hammered infrared
crescents: neon horseshoes for centaurs
galloping out of frame. But look, a young girl's

lonely survival in the hopeless forge of earth.
Unconventional kid who got how salvation means
drawing mustaches on masterpieces, offering
nuns posies that explode into poems.
Mona Lisa, Age Twelve: I might have been
looking in a mirror at her face. Kid smart-ass, her
big cagey smirk held up like a shield against it:
looming Womanhood, seductive lie after lie, sass-
mask of a tween sexless odd girl. Betting she can hold her own
against august fake mystery, one androgynous riddle of a smile!

Stay, Kate

—Catherine Sophia Blake

Mr. Blake sees God's face in the window
near a tree of angels, where he first
spies Kate flying. Many call him mad, he admits,

asking for her pity, which she gives. He
thanks her with his L-O-V-E. He prints
each letter, eager to show her the code,

as she is illiterate. He draws a wild-eyed
angel caressing another, amorous. Again,
she pities him, so she signs a marriage

contract with her "X." He teaches her. Angels
floating in a tree come from Innocence,
not Experience, signifiers of Law

and Justice and Lying Piety—negating Mercy,
its radiant human face. Beyond the burning gate
he imitates nothing from Knowledge (engraving his

genius terror-dreams, his dominion in a flash
of sand). When they are near starvation, not a single
painting sold—she sets an empty plate on the table,

trusting the dish will fill with illuminated fruit, celestial
drink. Yet, "I have little of Mr. Blake's company. He is
always in Paradise." (of the eternal rose.) Now

petals fall by his deathbed. He memorizes
her, as he rises up, asks for his drawing-pad.
"Stay, Kate." A sketch will make her eternal: his

hand poised. But the remaining mark is an "X,"
signifier of Kate All-Knowing, All-staying, deathless.

Rose

When her sister, my mother, flew far away
into herself, she came to us in her white-winged
head nurse's cap. Those in-charge eyes, signaling

her intent to thin us out like a late-night ER.
Her laws of *triage*—all the boys & one girl:
least likely to survive. Yet she kept administering

the sunrise: head wounds first. Had to admire that
victor spirit, not beaten down by birth after birth, like
her half-cracked sibling, shouting poems till syringefuls took.

Myself, I skated in perilous circles over a screaming
face just visible—below the surface of scarred ice.
Spinning ever inward, till she took me along
on the Vista Dome to that posh palmy Chicago
hotel, left me alone in the lamplit room where I still

endure an endless night. But her return, at dawn, meant
she was free, even of me. A free woman, a force I could
imitate: with a hatpin slid into a sleeve, set to impale

a stalker's eye. I cruised the du Maurier mysteries she
kept in her bookshelf, near the vanity mirror where I watched
her puff on filterless Camels. I hid-read her medical texts,

alarmed enough by what I saw there to spend years fleeing
the bloody facts of life. Before what happened (head wounds
first!) to her, eventually, would inevitably happen to me.

III.

Thomas at the Top (at Monticello)

—for Lisa Russ Spaar

We climbed the steep hidden stairway to
Jefferson's "brain," the octagon at the
very top, its clear panes round as eyes.
"Mars yellow" walls, sunlit green floor.
Imagining we could see what he once
saw: ". . . sublime to look down into the
workhouse of Nature . . . all fabricated at our feet."
Fabricated, in fact, all that plantation weather, in
the workhouse of the slave shacks below. Below
the dome, the house ticking as the Great Clock ticked,
the wind plate weathervane spun over dumbwaiters,
swing doors, multiple pens of his "copying machine."

Powerhouse running on beautifully-forged chains. Brain
that invented democracy copying theories of its opposite:
those pens attached to no hand, inking in rows of speculate
tyranny. What he saw from on top: a leap into our own
century, our twittering net of flailing nature. Justice still
random but unforeseen "online" mobs rising. Though
in foresight, said he'd "get a machine for scolding invented,"
get a machine to run on calumny. "Because it is a business
not fit for any human heart." He believed he knew what
was fit for us, our human hearts, because he viewed it
all from above. From his house, that shining machine,
running on its perfect architecture,
perfect invention, built on its foundation
of perfect wrong. Thomas at the top.

Mark Twain's Dream

He saw his own death riding the tail
of the Great Comet. Then bet on how
he'd end the way he came in: on

the back of a fireball. But when
he dreamt his brother in that coffin
resting on two chairs, with white

roses on his chest, one red in the
middle—he woke shouting & would
not rest until he saw Henry safe. So

the life of a young steamboat pilot
was like a former life, remembering
how to steer the sky, that reflection

on the water—"like the space where
a cloud had been," he wrote. But the
cloud sailed, the day dawned again,

Henry's boat blew sky-high. When
Sam came to find him, Henry lay
in a coffin resting on two chairs.

Sam, looking for the roses, saw a
nurse entering with his prophecy
in her hands. There the white petals,

there the blood-center, fireball &
heart: the red rose. Like a dream of
depth, surface to twain, that space where
                              a cloud had been.

Creation Myth

"We can die by it, if not live by love."
—John Donne

Super bewildered up there now, God wonders:
Should he have let the devil have his slippery
way, back there in the garden? Should he have

allowed Satan to arm Adam & Eve at the outset?
Should he have accepted the wager: that in no time
they'd zero in on each other—shooting like snipers

from the Tree of Knowledge? & if they managed
to breed—how long before the bros, Cain & Abel
shouldered their AR15s in the cradle & sped up

fratricide? Naturally, Noah would pick them
off (two by two, with a .22, right between the eyes)—
each species, mounting their heads inside the ark.

(Though he'd keep the sister wives afloat, to brag to.)
So there'd be no future without bees, birds, orangutans
& ten-toed sloths. Yet they'd keep their holy book
promising hellfire. What a joke they are, Satan
laughs. Whatever possessed you to give these lumps
of mud breath in the first place? Did you think

they'd sculpt "Art" out of the arsenal I lent them?
Did you think they'd keep on talking about Love—
after I dropped by Eden, offering the bloody lucky

                                dreams of Death?

Gun Control: a Triptych

I.

When the older brother, horsing around, opened fire
with the 12-gauge and shot his little brother in the back,
my Aunt Anna pressed her open

hand over the wound, over the blown right lung.
Blood stuttered up
through her fingers. As he began to slide away,
she kept
her hand flat-hard against that death.
At Emergency, they had to pry

it away. He survived that night.
When he takes his shirt off today, at the lake,
you can see the bleach-white stretch where
no hair grows and the skin thins to
her imprint—a hand-span—just under his shoulder.
Where a wing, if we had wings, might begin to unfurl.

2.

Blood hour. Hour of the startled bird
brought down in a field of first thoughts.
Trigger-quick. You can't know another mind,

but a teacher's job is showing each one how
to remake fate: fluttering up from the nest in
sudden flight. She prints each name in chalk:

each kid waves a wand. Bubbles! Faces
afloat in prisms. Then the one All-Fate, in-
escapable, exploding: camouflage figure, rifle.

Shouting into the room, his shouting mouth.
She has always believed that each soul
confronts the Unknown alone. Now she

sees It loaded, facing her. She calls out their
names, but their cries rise like birdcall, then
descend, one by one. What she's always loved:

their names. And it is almost Story Time, she
dreams, dying. The story today is Blood Hour.

3.

Some say it's High Noon in a big hat, shooting
up the saloon. America? Some say it's your

Second Amendment, those stockpiles of ammo
bought at a chain. Or the next-door kid living in

screen games: exploding heads, walking dead?
Or it's gangs in torched neighborhoods, drugs

running in the brain or a bead drawn on a clinic
doctor, women in line next to a homeless vet,

begging. Some say it's armed revolt, racist cops,
bragging hunters, looter-tools, mass crave/rave

for oblivion: Rapture addicts! Here comes one
more drive-by, school invasion, nightclub terror,

bully/bullied, lynch mob, god cult, toddler-a-cide.
O America, shooting from the hip, from the last of

the trees in a national park, your militia surrounded
by SWAT. Say you're an upstanding patriot in an

invented war—defending unborn lobbyists, a double-
sided coin minted by the National Reprisal Association

of the craven congressionals—saying it to history's
final judge. You, great god Gun, in whom some trust:

in bunker-mind, underground condos. O say it in Homeric
chanted dactyls: I sing of arms & the punk self-pumped-

up lovers of the Silencer. Dickinson wrote it first,
living god of Gun, you are "without the power to die."

Judge

Once, my big brother embodied
Justice. Once a wild teen, indifferent cadet,
reformed at last by the heavy weight of our
father's hand. *How it was done, then.* Maybe

why as the eldest son, he chose Law, then
presided over a courtroom filled with the lost
young. The day my mother & I visited, we sat
in the back, watching his altered face, both

attentive to testimony & turned away, as if
listening to or seeing something unheard, un-
seen by the rest of us. Invisible codex, on
a white wall, vanishing. *How it is done then, now.*

The strain of it, unlike the sweet swift pour
of mercy. Human failure in its signs:
character halfway doomed. Yet—
We are all only halfway saved. We watched her,

the woman appearing suddenly before him, her
young son beside her. She: crying out her life's worth
of tears. The boy in a motorcycle jacket, its pirate
flag boosting his pale defeated swagger. (Twelve,

thirteen?) *I have no choice,* she said. The boy suddenly loud:
I'll change. I promise. Single mother: how many
jobs? Gangs have stolen from her. Someone gave her son
a gun. He threatened a stranger, then threw it away. The judge,

my brother, asks for an answer. The boy kneels before her.
Don't do this. She turns away. Never had choice
in her life. She chooses now. The judge rules, she looks
away as guards escort him to his future.

Maybe this future, today, where my brother retains
his Fundamentalist denial of what I, on the
other side, find inalienable. The blind lady's scales tilt right,
tilt left. In that far past I watch the boy's mother exiting

past my mother & me. Her face a mask of agony & grief
I see reflected suddenly on the judge's face as he gavels away
the court's murmuring. I don't know when he turned forever
from the radiant Code, but the cases kept coming, standing before him.

Translation Class

—Rainer Maria Rilke, "Archaic Torso of Apollo"

The word's *augapfel*—
meaning eyeballs or "apple of the eye."

But we only have the torso of a god here.
Apollo's abs! Not, the poet writes, his

"unknowable" head. Not his unseen immortal gaze.

But a god might materialize within a sudden turn of phrase:
    those startled eyes,

arms and legs: sudden lamp-bright rays
       from inside the bruised translucence of stone.

Then a "proud manhood" flaring—don't look away!
See, this god doesn't lust after your little life—or care.
It is his own Apollonian god-ness insisting on itself,
handfuls of gems shaken over that chest, blinding

us. Blinking as each rendering slides its straitjacket
over him as he spins, rocketing back into monument.

Translation is about freeing ourselves from our selves:
That older voice, from the back.

Long ago Dresden, she sat, a kid in kitchen lamplight,
a decade after nonstop bombs obliterated each *strasse*:
        homes, hospitals, museums, towers: rotating

beams. She cut open an apple with a pocketknife,
watching its heart break into a five-pointed star,
                    that children then called *augapfel*.

Apple on a plate, Apollo's petaled eye . . .
Searchlights rake each word's perfect precedence.
There is nothing here that does not see you—

your word-history in ego's funny destruction,
in linguist-selfies, a drone's drone-sight. So follow Apollo now!
            @ hashtag: *You Must Change Your Life.*

IV.

Wildfire Moon (Summer, L.A. 2016)

—for Bill Handley

Pale ash falls from
the sky. On the lanai,
a child finger paints

a big red sun, twin to
the one that burns
above: mirror on fire.

What does the sun see,
through pages of smoke?
Hills: gargoyles, winged.

The horizon brazen as
the great fool's gold
jet landing on sparkler

wheels. She catches it:
the revolving star atop
a police cruiser, reflecting

in a flash, the blood moon
coming up at dusk. Printing
her name in what we call

stardust. No one can look
for long into a burning
mirror: faces break up into

blood shards. Still her small
fingers work ash into a
pink soul-lit version of

a planet unlike ours, its
moon withdrawing into
lit craters. Witness how

she rises, even in this sullen
white downfall, watching over
the indelible realms of touch.

No one else will ever render it so,
a world on fire burning within this
world that her fingers summon tonight,

arriving wild-bright and never again.

Mayhem

"At last, the distinguished thing."
—Henry James

—for Dede Gardner

My mayhem, she wrote. As if she owned it.
As if you could own a poem, or trouble.
Like that doomed boy driving the Jeep
(christened the Thing): there was mayhem!
Shearing corners,
                    doomed & drunk.

You're only a rider, somebody said.
A pilot shifts with the wind.
But you, you're just shotgun.

My mayhem drove the car, she
repeated from the death seat.
Maybe you think men ride differently
                    into it?

Not the "girl's" way: hand on his hand
on the gearshift. Not the "girl's" way,
long hair blowing, sidekick glance:

Never straight into what's coming?
Our windshield's panorama stops cold there,
that painted scene forming breath-colored:
            Snow in a poet's mouth. You could spell it out—
word for word, say it was impossible to make real,
                    yet it was made real.

Atop that cliff, where
the chassis shudders, begins
to roll, rolling over itself into

totaled. So the broken lilies
already appearing on its grave,
begin to blow west under the earth

under all that revs up, dies &
flowers,
            flowers & dies.

I made it be. So the Master
watching the snow through
         one bright window,

glances at the vase of spotlit
lilies floating to his pillow.
Turning toward it there on

his deathbed—the perfect
wrong word. Yes, he says.
  At last:

Workshop

They signed up for my poetry class, got passes
to travel from the cells to the cramped room
down the hall from the warden. Some "high profile"
(Assata S. or the girl who took the coke rap
for Abbie Hoffman)—but most not. Most deeply
preoccupied women writing poems of despair,
long letters to their court-stolen kids. Pages of
rant or reason. Most in for "victimless" raps:
hooking or boosting. The planes from La-
Guardia, across the water, roared over every four
minutes, so their handwriting shook like the walls
of this Women's House. Looping jazz blasting in
the halls kept up like an infant's nonstop crying. All
poems were written in pencil, since pens (the C.O.
said) could be made into weapons. Called contraband.
Pencils allowed for second chances, erased false starts.
Yet they pressed down hard anyway. They were poets
and that was the hope: that their words would last.

The Link

At six, she made potions: churned
mixes of mud & baking soda,
salts & rosewater—learning how
magic relies on manipulation
of expectation, science on proof.

At nine, she picked a budding rose from
our garden. Drops of dye from her vial
floated in the water glass where a white rose
slowly inhaled, till its petal edges were tinted
and the heart of the opening flower swirled blue.

The trees watched, as they watch always,
inhaling the world we've made. She learned
osmosis, as osmosis so long ago learned us. Now

I am near the end of my life, about to swallow
the last poison, the end of the end. Forget the
melodrama. But what will the future do, in the
birdless desert where the earth keeps trying to

breathe? & Science, as humans learn it, goes on
extrapolating from the rose to the alveoli connected to
the linked chain of being—& who will at last reveal those
links to the crowds expecting magic, roaring for magic—
                    in the face of the hard-to-swallow proof?

Seminar: Zebra Fish

—Prof. Rob Maxson

In the dark the screen lights up like an aquarium.
The fish move dreamily, their skulls gaping in places
traced in neon green & violet dye. A young woman stands,

waves an infrared wand, outlining mutations she's made,
making these unfused brain caps by scissoring a gene
named "Twist 1" & here it is: an altered future showing

up in the see-through embryo sac! So something made
wrong with these fish will make something right—like
heal the crania of human children born this way. Look,

our species can't regenerate itself or re-fuse, as zebra fish
can. We sicken, die, blame gods of luck or fate. But this silver
& blue striped female, this gold & blue striped male: they know

how to grow back a heart! They start it beating again—just
as they can rebirth a brain! The mutants swim before
our eyes, their lethal-looking wounds unwinding from super

genes, spliced. For the rest of us, death's still the same. Coffee
tastes as bitter today as tomorrow & screen light swims across
our eyes glimpsing images of dizzying prediction, turning

real. Who and what can be saved? Maybe we're not meant for
extinction. From real bad coffee, late seminars, to the young
woman with a wand, her gold, silver & blue shape-shifting fish,
there's a faint glow of hope from the genome. The screen pales,
darkens. Now it's time for the follow-up, time for further Q&A.

Microscope

"Fire thinks fire."
—Alice Fulton

Under a light microscope, a leaf is a leaf.
Under the transmission electron
microscope's eye that my daughter's eye

refines—a leaf's a landscape subatomic.
Particle choirs of light alter sight.
Electromagnetic lens held to a blink:

here in a world determined by its own
alienation from death. I remember, not
randomly, how they used to joke that

female smarts leaped, "scatterbrained." I
see her, a child, dyeing a rose from our garden
deep blue. I knew the world would always open

a hidden path for her. Rosalind F. first saw the
double helix as Photograph 51. The interlopers took
more than a cue from her slow-gathering lightning.

She was gone before this world recognized how
she'd first charted the cathedral. Stars slow by
entropy, by exclusion in her gaze. Now my daughter

scopes coal, fly-welter, airborne dust, ancient pine-
cone—each nano-narrative. Her alphabet begins as
minerals, fossil lint, then shaggy bacteria, wild wilder
virus. Half-skeptical, all the way back to The Bang.

"Fire thinks fire," I repeat, a charm against mutating
origins, but what do I know of these rippling souls

of elements, stripped to atomic ash on this ash planet,
this animate dust? To see in this light you must be
fearless. So I see only this: my blue rose,

                              my wonder.

Notes

"Rain": The hero of Novalis's novel *Heinrich von Ofterdingen* dreamed of a blue flower as the "holy miracle of nature." The blue flower or blue rose became a symbol of mystery in Romantic and intellectual thought, as well as a film motif (in David Lynch's television series *Twin Peaks*).

"Requiem for a Requiem": The modernist artist Paula Modersohn-Becker cried out in German, *"Schande!"* or *"Schade!"*, "Shame!" or "What a pity!", as she died of a postpartum embolism at the age of thirty-one with her newborn daughter in her arms.

"Failure to Thrive": "Failure to thrive" is a term used in pediatric medicine to indicate insufficient weight gain or inappropriate weight loss caused by medical problems or abuse or neglect (including deliberate starvation to preserve a childlike appearance).

"Audition": I briefly, embarrassingly, appeared in the rock musical *Hair* in Paris in 1970, in chorus and as the understudy to Crissy, the character who sings "Frank Mills."

"The Year the Law Changed": *Roe v. Wade*, the landmark Supreme Court case, was made law in 1973.

"Coolbrith: Homage": Poet Ina Coolbrith (1841–1928) was born Josephine Donna Smith, niece of the founder of Mormonism, Joseph Smith, to whom her mother was "sealed" (married to) after her husband's death. Coolbrith and her siblings fled polygamy with their mother, cross-country, after Smith's mob murder. Their Conestoga wagon crossed the Sierras with the help of the intrepid black

frontiersman James Beckwourth. Coolbrith was the first poet laureate of California, and the first poet laureate of any state.

"Adrienne": Includes lines from Adrienne Rich's poem "Moving in Winter."

"A Girl's Guide to the Epic": The United States Military Academy, West Point, invited poets to participate in a poetry reading series that lasted several years. Simone Weil described the epic *The Iliad* as a "poem of force," affecting both victors and vanquished.

"Ekphrasis": Fernando Botero's *Mona Lisa, Age Twelve*, 1959—a beguiling, large, preteen Mona Lisa.

"Translation Class": An unfortunate trend, in my view, of introducing the "self" of the translator into the translation process.

"Mayhem": Henry James's deathbed pronouncement: "At last, the distinguished thing."

"Workshop": In 1972, I founded a poetry and arts program at the Women's House of Detention on Rikers Island called "Art Without Walls/Free Space." The program expanded to Bedford Hills, Sing Sing, Attica, and prisons throughout New York State and continued for ten years.

"Seminar: Zebra Fish": I sat in on a seminar at the Keck School of Medicine of USC and learned a bit about the extraordinary, protean zebra fish, used widely in genetic research.

"Microscope": My daughter, Annie Muske-Dukes-Driggs, is a research scientist at Bend Research, Oregon. Her electron microscope images used in the frontispiece of this book are of a single rose petal, highly magnified. She says: "The rose petal was sputter-coated with gold palladium, then micrographs were captured on a Hitachi SU3500 Scanning Electron Microscope in SE mode."

Acknowledgments

Grateful thanks to my patient and inspired editor of so many years, Paul Slovak (and to Haley Swanson and Chris Smith). Thanks to all who have supported me as friends, advisors, or sympathizers in the long journey to *Blue Rose*. My gratitude (in random order) to: Grace Schulman, Suzanne Finstad, Jane Mead, Elizabeth Metzger, Cecilia Woloch, Susan Kinsolving, Lisa Russ Spaar, Debra Nystrom, Phillis Levin, Sophie Cabot Black, Bill Handley, Amy Schroeder, Dana Goodyear, David Roman, Francisco Espitia, and Emilie Golub. Finally, thanks to Kathy Muske, Kelsey Muske, and my sister Michele. Great gratitude to April Gornik, for "Untitled." (Finally, "Thanks, Mary!")

Grateful acknowledgment is made to the following publications, in whose pages these poems, or versions thereof, first appeared:

Academy of American Poets, Poem-a-Day, "Wildfire Moon"
Academy of American Poets, Poem-a-Day, "Failure to Thrive"
The American Poetry Review, "Kashmir: Hindu Doctor"
The Kenyon Review, "Mayhem"
Los Angeles Review of Books, "Requiem for a Requiem"
Milk Journal, "A Girl's Guide to the Epic"
T: The New York Times Style Magazine, "Live/Die"
The New York Times Magazine (forthcoming), "The Year the Law Changed"
The Paris Review, "No Hands"
Plume, "Audition"
Slate, "Gun Control"
Smithsonian, "Mark Twain's Dream"
The Yale Review, "Orphanage"

ANTHOLOGIES:

"Gun Control," in *Bullets into Bells: Poets and Citizens Respond to Gun Violence* (2017), edited by Brian Clements, Alexandra Teague, and Dean Rader

"Thomas at the Top" (as "Monticello"), in *Monticello in Mind: Fifty Contemporary Poems on Jefferson* (2016), edited by Lisa Russ Spaar

"Some Say," in *Resistance, Rebellion, Life: Fifty Poems Now* (2017), edited by Amit Majmudar

Photo: Kelsey Muske

Carol Muske-Dukes is the author of eight books of poetry (including *Sparrow*, a finalist for the National Book Award), four novels, and two collections of essays. She is a professor of English and Creative Writing at the University of Southern California, where she founded and was a former director of the PhD program in Creative Writing and Literature. Muske-Dukes is the former poet laureate of California and poetry columnist for the *Los Angeles Times Book Review*. She is the recipient of numerous awards and honors, including grants from the Guggenheim Foundation, the Ingram Merrill Foundation, and the National Endowment for the Arts; the 2012 Barnes & Noble Writers for Writers Award; and the Alice Fay Di Castagnola Award from the Poetry Society of America. Her work has been widely anthologized, including in *Best American Poetry*, the Pushcart Prize anthologies, and *The Penguin Anthology of Twentieth-Century American Poetry*. She lives in Los Angeles.

JOHN ASHBERY
Selected Poems
Self-Portrait in a Convex Mirror

PAUL BEATTY
Joker, Joker, Deuce

JOSHUA BENNETT
The Sobbing School

TED BERRIGAN
The Sonnets

LAUREN BERRY
The Lifting Dress

PHILIP BOOTH
Lifelines: Selected Poems 1950–1999

JULIANNE BUCHSBAUM
The Apothecary's Heir

JIM CARROLL
Fear of Dreaming: The Selected Poems
Living at the Movies
Void of Course

ALISON HAWTHORNE DEMING
Genius Loci
Rope
Stairway to Heaven

CARL DENNIS
Another Reason
Callings
New and Selected Poems 1974–2004
Night School
Practical Gods
Ranking the Wishes
Unknown Friends

DIANE DI PRIMA
Loba

STUART DISCHELL
Dig Safe

STEPHEN DOBYNS
Velocities: New and Selected Poems: 1966–1992

EDWARD DORN
Way More West

ROGER FANNING
The Middle Ages

ADAM FOULDS
The Broken Word

CARRIE FOUNTAIN
Burn Lake
Instant Winner

AMY GERSTLER
Crown of Weeds
Dearest Creature
Ghost Girl
Medicine
Nerve Storm
Scattered at Sea

EUGENE GLORIA
Drivers at the Short-Time Motel
Hoodlum Birds
My Favorite Warlord

DEBORA GREGER
By Herself
Desert Fathers, Uranium Daughters
God
In Darwin's Room

Men, Women, and Ghosts
Western Art

TERRANCE HAYES
Hip Logic
How to Be Drawn
Lighthead
Wind in a Box

NATHAN HOKS
The Narrow Circle

ROBERT HUNTER
Sentinel and Other Poems

MARY KARR
Viper Rum

JACK KEROUAC
Book of Blues
Book of Haikus
Book of Sketches

JOANNA KLINK
Circadian
Excerpts from a Secret Prophecy
Raptus

JOANNE KYGER
As Ever: Selected Poems

ANN LAUTERBACH
Hum
If in Time: Selected Poems, 1975–2000
On a Stair
Or to Begin Again
Under the Sign

CORINNE LEE
Plenty

PHILLIS LEVIN
May Day
Mercury
Mr. Memory & Other Poems

PATRICIA LOCKWOOD
Motherland Fatherland Homeland-sexuals

WILLIAM LOGAN
Macbeth in Venice
Madame X
Rift of Light
Strange Flesh
The Whispering Gallery

ADRIAN MATEJKA
The Big Smoke
Map to the Stars
Mixology

MICHAEL MCCLURE
Huge Dreams: San Francisco and Beat Poems

ROSE MCLARNEY
Its Day Being Gone

DAVID MELTZER
David's Copy: The Selected Poems of David Meltzer

ROBERT MORGAN
Dark Energy
Terroir

CAROL MUSKE-DUKES
Blue Rose
An Octave Above Thunder

Red Trousseau
Twin Cities

ALICE NOTLEY
Certain Magical Acts
Culture of One
The Descent of Alette
Disobedience
In the Pines
Mysteries of Small Houses

WILLIE PERDOMO
The Essential Hits of Shorty Bon Bo

LIA PURPURA
It Shouldn't Have Been Beautiful

LAWRENCE RAAB
The History of Forgetting
Visible Signs: New and Selected Poems

BARBARA RAS
The Last Skin
One Hidden Stuff

MICHAEL ROBBINS
Alien vs. Predator
The Second Sex

PATTIANN ROGERS
Generations
Holy Heathen Rhapsody
Quickening Fields
Wayfare

SAM SAX
Madness

ROBYN SCHIFF
A Woman of Property

WILLIAM STOBB
Absentia
Nervous Systems

TRYFON TOLIDES
An Almost Pure Empty Walking

SARAH VAP
Viability

ANNE WALDMAN
Gossamurmur
Kill or Cure
Manatee/Humanity
Structure of the World Compared to a Bubble

JAMES WELCH
Riding the Earthboy 40

PHILIP WHALEN
Overtime: Selected Poems

ROBERT WRIGLEY
Anatomy of Melancholy and Other Poems
Beautiful Country
Box
Earthly Meditations: New and Selected Poems
Lives of the Animals
Reign of Snakes

MARK YAKICH
The Importance of Peeling Potatoe Ukraine
Unrelated Individuals Forming a Group Waiting to Cross

MAY - - 2018